Keeping up appearances!
The words have perhaps, a rather a terrifying
sound, implying a smiling face to the world and a
bare cupboard at home; but really and truly if one
goes sensibly to work, keeping up appearances need
mean nothing of the sort. 1899

In the store-room

APPEARANCES
HOW TO KEEP THEM UP ON A LIMITED INCOME

From an original 1899 book of advice

Copper Beech Publishing

Appearances – how to keep them up

Published in Great Britain by
Copper Beech Publishing Ltd
© Copper Beech Publishing Ltd 2002

ISBN 1-898617-33-3

A CIP catalogue record for this book is available from The British Library.

Copper Beech Gift Books
Copper Beech Publishing Ltd
P O Box 159 East Grinstead
Sussex England RH19 4FS

A small income is no excuse for
a soiled tablecloth.

KEEPING UP APPEARANCES

There is a good and a bad side to keeping up appearances and all honour should be done to the woman who extracts the greatest comfort and daintiness out of a small income.

Take those three most important things in daily life – food, servants and dress.

three
important
things

Food

It costs no more, perhaps rather less, to have dainty, well served meals than it does to make shift with a pound of cooked beef and a bottle of indigestible pickles.

It costs no more, but it does call for untiring and increasing energy on the part of the housewife.

Servants

It means taking pains and using infinite patience
when training your cook at £10 a year.

It means teaching, teaching, teaching, every time
you come in contact with your helper at 2s a week
to turn her into a neat-handed house-parlourmaid.

Dress

A small income is no excuse for a slovenly servant.
The wages of a clean, neat girl are not higher than
those of a slattern, and it won't cost you a single
penny more to feed her either.

slovenly

A careful girl should be able to make three afternoon aprons, and one or two smart caps, last her a
week at least.

When you have a caller for afternoon tea, you may not be able to afford tennis cake or the latest thing in sweet biscuits, but the bread and butter can be daintily cut and rolled, the tea well and freshly made, and the hot water jug filled with absolutely boiling water.

The tea tray, even though it may lack silver, can be daintily set, and if the maid who carries it in can be smart, clean and wholesome to look at, depend upon it, the cake will never be missed!

The little things

comfort When all these little items (which, though small in themselves, go to make up the grand total of daily comfort or discomfort) are studied as they should be, keeping up appearances need not prove such a difficult thing after all.

WAYS AND MEANS ON £300 A YEAR

£300 a year isn't a very large sum, especially when it has to provide not only house, food, firing and lights, but clothing, amusements, pocket money, and the hundred-and-one incidental expenses of daily life.

Finding a House
To describe an average house; on the ground floor is a good sized dining-room, and at the back another room, which could form an admirable study.

The basement will contain coal cellars, dustbin, a kitchen of fair size, a breakfast room, and a scullery with a copper. With a copper the washing bill can be kept at bay! In addition to the scullery is usually a yard, dreary enough perhaps, but:

'Quite good enough to dry clothes in.'

marble

Upstairs is a drawing-room capable of holding forty or fifty people at an evening party quite comfortably. Upstairs again for preference, four good bedrooms, a dressing-room, with marble lavatory fitment, a bath-room, with hot and cold water, and the usual offices.

Before you finally decide to take a house, call in an expert opinion as to the drains, &c. and have them thoroughly tested. The money spent should never be begrudged, as it is the one and only means of avoiding serious illness. You will need to allow for taxes and water rates.

table of expenses

Allow in your 'table of expenses' for coals, gas and the servants' wages. Provide also for clothes, travelling expenses, pocket-money and annual holidays; you must bank some savings.

FURNISHING

Do not overcrowd
In furnishing, do not make the fatal mistake of
overcrowding the rooms with furniture, and don't
go in for hangings of any sort, except the harmless
necessary short and long curtains.

mistake

Hangings
Hangings of all sorts are unhealthy and, unless one
wishes one's house to have a tawdry, ill-kempt and
ill-kept appearance, these things add to that bug-
bear, the washing bill, to no inconsiderable extent.

ill-kept
appearance

IN SEARCH OF SERVANTS

As soon as you are married, and have got your house in decent order, set about finding the servants wherewith to 'run it.'

A drudge

two
domestics

There can be no real comfort, no good cooking, unless the woman is prepared to degenerate into a household drudge and do it all herself. There will be no daintiness, unless you keep two domestics.

At first you can take dinner at restaurants, a different one every night, but you will rapidly tire of this, because expensive meals are beyond your means.

TRAINING

Be gentle
To have ill-trained and careless servants is nothing less than disgraceful. When training a young girl, take care not to lose your temper. Force yourself to be gentle, no matter how distasteful the effort may be.

Explain, over and over again, and never allow a fault, either in waiting, answering the door, or speaking, pass unchecked. Little faults will grow into big ones, and to crop up and humiliate you.

little faults

Familiarity
Don't let her 'forget her cap' or forget to bring letters and telegrams on a waiter. Above all, never allow any familiarity. With the cook, be equally careful.

YOUR CHARWOMAN

*Mrs.
Charwoman*

Up until now you will have been dependent upon the services of a charwoman who, for a consideration, has consented to come and 'do' pending the arrival of the domestics.

Many prepare breakfast and lunch, and after washing up the luncheon things, leave for the rest of the day to make some other family 'comfortable.'

THE SERVANTS' FIRST DAY

Preparing for the servants' first day

*cleanliness
and
order*

Arrange for your new servants to enter on a Monday evening and that day make yourself busy, aided by Mrs. Charwoman, who will restore everything to a state of exquisite cleanliness and order.

Your work

Your part of the work should be as follows:- First
make a list of the entire contents of the linen press,
then of the glass and china cupboards and finally
of the silver. Then make a duplicate copy of each
list in a little penny book, to be handed to the new
maid when she arrives.

a
little
book

Purchase two large sheets of white cardboard and
upon these draw up a list of the duties you expect
each maid to perform, dividing them into 'Every-
day Duties' and 'Special Duties.'

By adopting this plan you will do away at once with
any chance of disputes between them.

One of these cards then – the cook's – can be nailed
up behind the kitchen door, the other secured to
the door of the glass cupboard.

17

When the maids have arrived, show them to their bed-room, give them just time to take off their things, and then take them on a tour of the house.

Finally, give cook her orders for the next day's breakfast, and tell them that as they will find all their work clearly written out, there is no need to detain them any longer.

In the store room

COOK'S DUTIES

Mornings: Light kitchen fire. Sweep hall, dining-room, study, and lavatory. Clean grates and light other fires. While dust settles, clean door-steps and brasses. Dust hall, dining-room, study and lavatory. Prepare and have own breakfast. Tidy kitchen. Take orders for day. Attend to special duties for day. Prepare lunch for kitchen and dining-room.

After lunch: Wash up. Clean kitchen. Tidy scullery. Attend to special duties if any. Have own tea. After tea: Prepare dining-room dinner. Afterwards have own dinner. Wash up. Tidy kitchen and scullery for night.

COOK'S SPECIAL DUTIES

Mondays – Do washing. Clothes to be put to soak on Sunday night.

Tuesdays – Clean all brasses and kitchen brights. Turn out store cupboards and pantries.

Wednesdays – Do ironing and own mending.

Thursdays – Turn out dining-room. (Housemaid helps).

Fridays – Turn out study, hall, lavatory, and servants' bed-room.

Saturdays – Turn out and clean thoroughly kitchen, scullery, area passages and steps, and sweep yard. Be dressed by four o'clock.

Nights out, every other Sunday. One evening per week.

HOUSE PARLOURMAID'S DUTIES

Mornings: Sweep and dust stairs. Take hot water, tea and letters to mistress's bed-room. Take hot water to master's dressing-room. Sweep and dust drawing-room. Clean boots and knives. Lay dining-room for breakfast, and kitchen. Have own breakfast. Serve dining-room breakfast. Strip beds. Empty slops. Make beds. Sweep and dust bed-rooms and bath-room. Wash up breakfast things. Attend to special duties. Lay kitchen and dining-room lunch. Dress. Wait at lunch. Have own lunch.

After lunch: Clear away dining-room and kitchen luncheon things, and wash up all silver, glass, and china. Make and serve afternoon tea. Lay kitchen tea. Have own tea.

After tea: Wash up all tea things, silver, &c. Lay dining-room and kitchen dinner. Take hot water to bed and dressing-rooms. Serve dining-room dinner and wait at table. After dining-room dinner, have own dinner. Clear away dining-room dinner things, and wash up all glass, silver and china. Tidy bed-rooms for night. Turn down beds. Take hot water to bed-rooms.

SPECIAL DUTIES

Mondays – Do all house mending. Tuesdays – Turn out drawing-room. Wednesdays – Clean glass cupboard and all the silver. Thursdays – Turn out spare bed-rooms. Fridays – Turn out mistress's bed-room and dressing-room. Saturdays – Do mistress's mending. Be dressed by one o'clock. Nights out every other Sunday. One evening per week.

DOMESTIC DETAILS – THE COOK

Firstly, explain to your new cook that you intend to send in, every Saturday, sufficient stores to last the week out. Say in a pleasant voice:

sufficient stores

'I always allowance my servants, because I find it works so much better, and then I always know exactly how much is required. I shall allow you quarter of a pound of tea, a pound of sugar, and half a pound of butter each. I only allow the same quantity for your master and myself, so you see you are being treated with absolute fairness. I expect all these, and whatever other stores I send in, to last the whole week and if there is any deficiency I shall expect you to make it good. Of course, I always make an extra allowance when we have a luncheon or dinner party.'

Be brave; even if you expect your newly-acquired
domestic treasure to give notice on the spot. She
will almost surely smile, and say pleasantly:

domestic
treasure

'Oh! I'll make them last all right, madam.'

Then you must go on:

'You must save all the fat from the top of the soup and
the joints, and once a week we will clarify it, and then it
will be fit for use as a frying medium. Do you know
how to clarify fat?'

If she does not, make a mental note to teach her to
clarify fat and make stock, as a starting-point. Then
continue:

a
mental
note

'Just one thing more, never throw away anything, no

matter if it's only a bit of cold cabbage or potato, or a scrap of bacon rind, until you've shown it to me. When I've trained you, and turned you into a good cook, as I hope to do, you can use your own discretion then, but in these, your learning days, you must come to me with everything.'

After this leave her to cook her first lunch for you in undisturbed peace. You will want to find out exactly how much she actually does or does not know.

It is also advisable to purchase a couple of smart aprons for cook, for such times as she should take her turn in attending to the door, for when you have your little monthly reception.

DOMESTIC DETAILS –
THE HOUSE-PARLOURMAID

Proceed to your house-parlour maid; say boldly:

*'I've written all your work out for you, as you see, so
that you know what you have to do, and now I'm going
to tell you just how to do it. Pay great attention to me,
and try and remember all I tell you.'*

attention

Then continue:

'Now I'm going to sit at this table' – (sit in the dining-room) – *'and I want you to imagine that I'm having my dinner, and that you're bringing me the vegetables. Now upon which side would you hand them?
The left, always the left.'*

always
the
left

Next, lay the cloth, explain where everything has to be put, the difference between fish knives and fruit knives and exactly how much water must be allowed to each finger-bowl. As soon as the table is laid to your satisfaction, make her strip it again. **repeat** Repeat this four or five times. By then she will do it correctly, greatly to her delight and yours!

When a month has passed
One month of training will turn her into a creditable parlourmaid. She will occasionally make mistakes; correct these as they arise.

Announcing visitors
visitors Next day, put her through her paces opening the front door, showing in and announcing visitors. She may make very droll mistakes, but in time she will learn to discriminate with the utmost nicety.

THE HOUSE – PARLOURMAID'S DRESS

Be very particular as to your house-parlourmaid's dress.

Morning
For mornings she should wear a gown of the darkest grey linen, with a broad white collar. Do not allow servants to wear light prints for the obvious reason that these increase the washing bill.

dark linen

Afternoons
For afternoons she must have the usual black gown with white cuffs, collar and a smart white apron. It is impossible for her to purchase white aprons as well as clothe herself out of the two shillings per week you pay her, so find a cheap little draper who makes servants' aprons, and get half-a-dozen or so.

29

Caps and cuffs
Simple ones will be quite pretty enough to please the most fastidious. In addition to these, buy a single very smart one for wear on reception days, or when you have people to dinner. You can obtain caps cheaply, but these will not boast 'streamers,' and though the latter may be highly fashionable, make up your mind to forego them.

most fastidious

Except on very special occasions, make shift with paper cuffs, because you can get six pairs at a reasonable price and really they look every bit as nice as their more costly brethren fashioned of linen.

No one ever wants to visit people who are perpetually hard up, but no one who keeps within his income, be it even but a halfpenny to the good, can be said to be in this unpleasant predicament.

'Half soiled cap strings, are worse than no caps
strings at all.'

THE LARDER

caviar

With limited means, anything in the nature of a store cupboard worthy of the name will be quite out of the question. Caviar, pate de foie gras, fonds d'artichauts, glacé cherries, and all other delicacies – which are such a help towards providing dainties in an emergency – are beyond reach.

Check your stores

store
cupboard

Every Saturday before going shopping examine your store's contents carefully, and replace those of your 'stores' which show signs of running out. Whenever you find yourself possessed of a spare shilling, always expend it in the replenishment of the cupboard, and by degrees you will get together a host of dainties which are simply invaluable when you have people to dine or to augment the dinner.

Basics

The foundation of your store cupboard should include: Rice – buy the less expensive variety, it is quite as good as that which is dearer, but it is smaller grained and requires a great deal of washing. Tapioca, semolina, sago, red lentils, butter beans, a bottle of soy, vanilla essence, jelly crystals, essence of rennet (for making junkets) chutney, mustard, anchovy paste, bloater paste, raisins, currants, candied peel, golden syrup, cooking jam, marmalade, vinegar, oil, tarragon vinegar, a bottle of mushroom catsup, pickled walnuts, bottle of olives, box of brown desiccated soup, dried mint, sage and sweet herbs, bay leaves, cloves, cinnamon, mace, nutmeg, allspice, broken sweet biscuits (these latter for puddings, but only to be used for a dinner party), preserved ginger, barley, garlic, shallots.

KEEPING A HOUSE SWEET AND CLEAN

You must remember that to keep a house really sweet and clean, one requires a plenitude of such things as soap, soda, beeswax, turpentine, hearthstone and blacklead.

Soda
It is by far the cheapest to buy soda in the 6d. bags, these contain 28 lbs. But if you wish to be successfully economical you must not let your maid have the whole bag at once! If you do, the best part of that soda will find its way down the kitchen sink, for she will take a handful when a bit the size of a walnut is all that is required.
Some suggest that you tell maids how soda coarsens and reddens the hands.

Furniture polish

Don't buy furniture polish or cream. For ordinary and oak furniture turpentine and beeswax is by far the cheapest polishing medium you can employ, and articles of furniture which have been French polished, if well rubbed up with an old silk handkerchief, should not require any other polish.

Brass

There is nothing better than a little of one of the numerous brass polishes sold now. Use this polish sparingly as, if imperfectly rubbed off, it will produce verdigris and in the end the article in question will look worse instead of better.

verdigris

Silver

For cleaning silver, nothing can excel ordinary whitening mixed to a paste by means of a little water, methylated spirits, or gin, though the latter adds a trifle to the expense it will make such a fine polish.

Looking glasses
Looking glasses requiring a special cleaning should be damped with a little methylated spirits and then well polished with an old silk handkerchief. A little vinegar (only a few drops are required) added to the cold water in which the table glass is rinsed will brighten and make it easier to polish.

silk handkerchief

Knives
For cleaning knives, finely powdered bath brick answers quite as well as knife polish. It may be urged that this tends to scratch the steel, but if rubbed only backwards and forwards instead of up and down all ways, this is not the case.

Steps

For the front door steps, whitening is to be preferred to hearthstone as it gives a much better colour and dries more quickly.

front steps

Windows

For the windows, always have a leather to give the final polish when cleaning. A cloth is apt to leave unsightly bits of fluff behind it and make the windows look as though the cleaning had been very imperfectly done indeed.

leather

Boots

Boot cream can represent a large part of your cleaning budget. Try beeswax and turpentine next time; it will be found to answer equally well, but requires plenty of elbow grease to put as fine a polish on to even the dullest pair of patent leather boots.

elbow grease

Carpets
If carpets have got dull and faded looking, try rubbing them with a cloth wrung out of tepid water to which has been added a little ammonia, this will fetch up the colour.

Soap
When buying soap, get half a dozen bars at a time, put it in a cool, dry place and let it dry slowly, soap thus hardened lasts twice as long.

Disinfectant

If you require a disinfectant at any time, there is nothing better or cheaper than a pennyworth of chloride of lime, and though this perhaps smells unpleasantly, the odour soon goes off and it does its work thoroughly and well.

Stove polishes

Buy the cheapest blacklead you can get. The so called 'stove polishes' with high sounding names have all blacklead as their basis, and you only pay extra for the name. You will find it cheaper in the long run to buy your turpentine and beeswax ready mixed, as less is required when it is of the right creamy consistency.

SPRING CLEANING

muddle

Do not indulge in a regular spring cleaning unless you can afford to add the services of a charwoman. Otherwise, you will only get into a muddle and make everybody thoroughly uncomfortable.

Chimney sweeping

chimneys

Keep the house absolutely clean all year round, and when the time for leaving off fires occurs, let the sweep do one chimney per day, when that room has its usual weekly turning out. In this way you will put no extra work on your servants.

Carpet beating

Have the carpets beaten while you are away for your annual holiday. One of the tradesmen is generally glad to do this for an odd shilling or two.

HOW TO SPEND THE HOUSEKEEPING

How much?
How much should be allowed for food? And how much for the laundry bill? Draw up a table of what you actually must send out, and keep to it, not exceeding it by so much as a pocket-handkerchief.

budgeting

Healthy appetites
In your little note-book make note of laundry, fishmonger, egg merchant, baker. If you are four people, all blessed with healthy appetites, and there would be occasional callers at tea time, you can not reckon on less than two loaves a day.
Also make an allowance for the replenishment of the stock pot.

Store list
Make your store list. Of tea, you must have at least a pound, coffee you can not do without. If you both possess a sweet tooth, make a good allowance for sugar. Include cooking sugar too. A whole host of absolutely necessary things may make you decide to take a pound of your own money and stock a tiny cupboard which stands on one side of the kitchen as another store cupboard.

The greengrocer
At the greengrocer's shop, order sixpennyworth of potatoes, a cauliflower of quite large size, two pounds of apples to use for dessert, a lettuce, two pennyworth of onions, a pennyworth each of carrots and turnips – these latter for the betterment of the soup – together with a large cabbage.

Other tradesmen

Before wending your way to the stores full of glee, be sure that you have not forgotten the butcher, the florist and the milkman.

Of milk, a quart a day, taking a pint and a half in the mornings, and half a pint in the afternoons will be needed. Determine to pay the milkman every day to keep control of your various expenses.

By achieving various small economies now and again when you have been out to dinner a good deal, you will be able to keep level with everyone.

THE LAUNDRY BILL

The laundress

First, make a contract with the laundress to take the servants' washing at one shilling per head. Do this for two reasons. First and foremost because you want them always to look essentially smart, an impossibility if they go about in home-laundered print gowns, capes, cuffs, collars and aprons.

You may also feel – if you are ultra fastidious – that you do not quite like the idea of their under garments being washed together with your towels, serviettes, &c.

Husband's shirts

The next serious item on the laundry bill is a husband's shirts and collars. His underwear can be washed at home, but you will probably decide that he could not possibly do with less than a dozen collars per week (the extra ones allowed in view of a probable evening engagement), three shirts, and a like number of pairs of cuffs he must have; and then there will be your own linen.

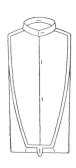

Table linen

Clean serviettes and tablecloths are a must, as these would soon be completely spoilt, and a single sideboard cloth and five o'clock tea cloth come under the heading of absolute necessities.

Decide that these could go once a fortnight, and so, too, could the frilled shams. These latter also call for the care of a well-trained laundress.

The d'oyleys need no 'getting up' in the ordinary sense of the word, and you can wash them out in the hand basin yourself.

Pocket-handkerchiefs, towels, sheets, counter-panes, bed-spreads, the art linen and household cloths of every description can also be done at home, as well as of course, the socks and stockings.

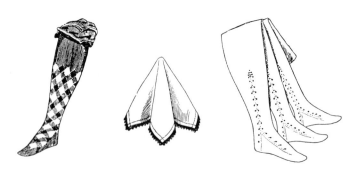

THE COOK – HOW TO TRAIN HER

Make friends with your cook. At the same time be very careful never to let her overstep the boundary between mistress and maid.

Sternest necessity
When you commence to train her, begin by taking her into your confidence, explaining that you are economical, not from choice, but from sternest necessity.

economical from necessity

Waste not a crumb
Most servants hate a mean mistress, but respect a careful one, and so take care to make yours understand, that while you do not intend to stint them, they must not waste even so much as a crumb while they are in your house.

careful

A small economy

If you are fortunate and your cook is naturally a good warm-hearted girl, she will readily fall into your ways, and whenever a small economy of any sort is practicable, she will always be eager to be the one to suggest it.

Culinary accomplishments

When she enters your service her culinary accomplishments will probably be: she can roast a joint very fairly, cook potatoes and the plainest greens, such as peas, cabbages, &c; make a custard, pancakes or tapioca pudding and also, she can probably concoct one kind of tea cake. Her sauces may be limited to a bread sauce of poultice-like consistency, and white sauce.

Probably she has never heard of French cookery and does not know the meaning of stock.

Explain to her that, where anything of a difficult nature is concerned, you will do it first, and then, giving her the recipe, shall expect her to follow it the next time without any assistance. Say:

'But, where anything fairly easy is in question, I shall expect you to manage without assistance from me. And bear in mind that if you attend to my instructions properly, and go by the recipe, you must be successful.'

Recipes
In addition to this, write out all the recipes you give her, in a plain round hand, and in the simplest manner and language you can command.

It is no use giving elaborately worded recipes to an inexperienced cook. It will only confuse her and serve no good purpose.

The second morning after your cook arrives, commence with your instructions, having gauged her capabilities by the luncheon and dinner she had cooked the day before.

The very first lesson should be in stock making.

stock
making

Recipe for stock making

Take a sufficient quantity of bones, sprinkle them liberally with salt, place on a clean dish, and then leave the dish in a hot oven for ten minutes. This browns the salt without cooking the meat left on the bones, and gives the soup a good colour. Next put the bones in a deep saucepan, and fill up with cold water. Place on the fire and bring gently to the boil. Then skim carefully. Add a bouquet garni

– this consists of bayleaf, a sprig of thyme and mar-
joram, and a sprig of parsley all tied together, a tiny
blade of mace, twenty or thirty peppercorns, and
half a dozen cloves and a little celery seed; do not
add either carrots, turnips, or onions to the first
boiling, as stock made thus turns sour far more
quickly – half a cupful of cold water, and salt to
taste. Draw the saucepan to the side of the fire,
and let it simmer gently for six or seven hours.
Every now and then you can remove the scum that
will arise, but you must not allow the stock to cook
quickly enough to reduce, or it will be spoilt. Then
drain it off through a sieve into a deep soup bowl,
and leave in the larder till next morning. By this
time there will be a thick cake of fat floating on the
top. Remove this and add to the fat pan to be clarified later. Take care that not a particle of fat is left
on the stock. Then use as necessary.

As soon as you have shown cook how to make stock, proceed to put her through her paces as regards the fat. Teach her how to utilise and clarify the dripping from the joints and soup.

How to clarify fat
Pour over the bowl containing the fat to be clarified enough boiling water to nearly fill it. Then leave in the larder till perfectly cold. When cold the cake of fat will be found on top. If it is very dirty – full of small brown specks – repeat the above process again. The fat is then fit for use. (The bottom of the cake may be lightly scraped in case any impurity still remains.)

Grilling

The only requisite for grilling properly is a perfectly clear fire.

The fire for grilling: make it up with cinders early in the afternoon, say about four o'clock. Leave the dampers out and by dinner time you should have an exquisitely clear red fire.

Avoid waste

Do not try to teach cook too many dishes at once. Here is a good plan. As soon as she gets on a little, and is to be trusted alone, give her two fresh recipes every day. For example, a new soup and say a new entrée, or a new fish dish and a new pudding. (Savouries do not count, as these are so easy.) Thus you are sure not to overload her intelligence in any way. It is always advisable to avoid confusing an inexperienced girl, and also avoid the mistakes and waste which are bound to result if she is confused.

Exercise great patience! You can not train a cook without it. Encourage her, too, to ask questions, and tell her the why and wherefore of everything.

waste

Cleanliness
Many girls who know but little of cookery are apt to be very careless as to cleanliness. This does not mean cleanliness in the ordinary sense of the word, but that they will go straight from handling fish to make a pudding or mix a salad!

A bowl of water
Cultivate good habits and always reserve a bowl full of water close at hand during cooking operations. Insist on your cook washing her hands as need arises. You will find that after a little drilling you will not have to dread your cutlets coming to table with a decidedly 'fishy' flavour about them.

As cook grows more and more experienced, you can indulge in rather more elaborate entrées that is, of course, when funds permit.

BREAKFASTS

With limited housekeeping money, to indulge in eggs and bacon every day is out of the question.

For your husband
For your husband something more substantial will be an absolute necessity.

variety

Remember that variety is the spice of life, so let this meal vary as much as possible. One morning give kidneys. Split, fry and fill the centre with a scrap of butter. What is left over will make a savoury for the evening's dinner if spread upon two tiny squares of toast.

Another morning, dried haddock with egg sauce can be served.

Another morning, have scrambled eggs.

Another, kippers or a bloater. When any fish is left from the previous night's dinner, turn it into fish cakes or into kedgeree; and on Sundays you can indulge in a small tin of smoked sardines.

Every morning serve porridge, sometimes made from oatmeal, or from Quaker oats. Marmalade should always be on hand, for most men like something sweet as a finish to breakfast.

Always insist upon a rack full of crisp golden brown toast, and what is left of this can reappear at dinner.

In the winter, you may wish to indulge in fried toast; this should go to table crisp, yet soft inside.

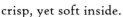

Hot cakes

Hot cakes sound extravagant, but are not so in reality. Add a good pinch of salt to half a pound of self raising flour, run in two ounces of clarified beef dripping, mix with a little milk and water, shape into rounds, bake in a fairly hot oven for half an hour, split, butter and serve. With the addition of two ounces of sugar and an extra two ounces of dripping, these will do excellently for afternoon tea; raisins, currants or a little spice may be added at discretion.

Bacon

the
best
bacon

Never economise when it comes to bacon. Insist on the best and the best only.

LUNCHEONS

If your husband is out all day, plan to have a meat luncheon as a rule only on Saturdays, when he is home for that meal.

On other days, have a thick substantial soup fol-lowed by a substantial pudding. Vary the soup each day and the pudding also.

Clear soup followed by a baked custard will not enable anybody to go from breakfast till dinner (tea does not count) without feeling hungry.

Turn all your scraps of vegetables to account so that nothing is wasted. Cold potatoes should not escape. Make a potato salad.

scraps

THE SERVANTS' MEALS

Mornings
Servants meals can be arranged like this. In the mornings they have tea or cocoa for breakfast, with as much bread and butter as they choose to eat, and an egg, or a kipper for relish on Sundays.

Luncheon
Their luncheon can be the same as yours.

Tea

For tea they could have a dripping cake hot or cold, if they choose to make it, or else a little golden syrup or jam with their bread and butter. Occasionally, too, when bloaters are cheap, they can have one apiece for tea.

Dinner
Their dinner can be the same as your own with the
sole exception of fruit and savouries. Never have
more than two or three of the latter made unless
you are expecting guests, as to relegate them to the
kitchen means throwing them away.

Fruit
You can not afford to buy fruit for the servants,
although now and again, when apples or oranges
are cheap, give them one each on Sundays.

fruit
on
Sundays

Waste and grumbling
By feeding them exactly as yourself, you prevent
two drawbacks to economical housekeeping: waste
and grumbling. Nothing is wasted because every
scrap is eaten up, and no servant can grumble if
she has the same fare as her master and mistress.

COPING WITH THE WASH AT HOME

To wash at home is not the easiest thing. This is how to manage it:

The week's plan
The clothes should all be all sorted on Saturday evenings, with the exception of the sheets. On Sunday night they should be put to soak in soapy water. On Monday morning, the fine white things, such as sheets, towels, pillow slips, and handkerchiefs must all be washed first. Then the flannels, and the dusters should be done afterwards in the lather from the sheets. This saves the soap.

The tea cloths, meat cloths, first cloths and glass cloths being, of course, done separately in fresh water.

Lighting the fire
The copper fire is always lighted the very first thing
in the morning, and by ten o'clock the first lot of
things should always be on to boil.

Hints for success
Don't use dark blue, the pale is to be preferred.
If you do starched things, add a pinch of powdered
borax in your starch.
To take ink, tea, or wine stains out of table linen,
nothing can excel salts or lemon.
A little paraffin added to the water in which the
dusters are put to soak, will help to get the dirt out
more quickly.
Never attempt to boil coloured and white things
together, or the results will be disastrous.
Never allow your maid on any pretext (save that
of illness) to leave any of the washing which is

already in the water and partly washed, over 'for next day,' if you do, your linen will soon be spoilt.

Use the lawn to bleach
If you possess a lawn, no matter how small, always utilise it to bleach the linen, nothing will make it such a good colour. It must be sprinkled occasionally from time to time as it gets over dry.

Ironing
Linen which has got over dry must also be sprinkled before ironed or mangled.

the
iron

When about to iron, test the iron with a bit of paper, this is much better than the old-fashioned way of holding the iron close to the face. The latter test may result in an accident if the maid is suddenly startled.

Well aired
Bear in mind also that clothes, when ironed, should not be put away until they have been thoroughly aired; if this is omitted, mildew is likely to result. Have the lines strung up in the kitchen, and see for yourself that all the clean things, but more especially the sheets, pillow slips, under-linen and flannels of every description are hung up and aired.

Never imagine that any amount of 'cleanser' will ever take the place of genuine rubbing, because it will not.

ENTERTAINING

The table
It is no more trouble to place things on to a table properly than it is to fling them on anyhow!

Smeary glassware

smeary glassware

Well polished glass and clean shining plates are within the reach of everybody. That your glass is but blown and not cut, is no excuse for its being sent to table in the condition known as 'smeary'.

Careless
Young and untrained servants can be careless in this respect, but one way to cure them of this is to send the article back to the kitchen then and there to be washed and repolished, no matter whether you have to wait for it or not.

FLOWERS

fresh
flowers

Always try to manage to save a few pence out of the housekeeping money for fresh flowers. Get a set of creamy white china vases, taking care to select those with very tiny necks. Change the water in the flower vases every day, and clip the ends of the stalks, but directly they show even the slightest sign of withering off they must go.

No table, let it be ever so spotless a cloth, and be never so daintily laid, can possibly look even passably nice if adorned with withered flowers.

A threepenny or sixpennyworth of flowers in small specimen vases if arranged with taste will have quite as good an effect as half a guinea's worth of costly blooms.

specimen vases

A MODEST DINNER

To give a dinner party with champagne, expensive liqueurs and with the table decorated by a fashionable florist, will, of course, be out of the power of those on limited means.

Served as they should be

never miss luxuries

You may not be able to afford bisques, salmon and whitebait, game and poultry, pineapples and black grapes, but if your simple purée is hot, the grilled herrings and mustard sauce cooked to a turn, and your stewed steak hot and nicely seasoned, your golden toast crisp and well drained, and if all these things are served as they should be, you will never miss luxuries.

Special occasions
If the occasion is an important one, serve a dish of petits vols au vents. For soup, have a well-made vegetable purée, enriching it for the occasion by the addition of a pennyworth of cream and the yolk of an egg. Follow with a roast shoulder of mutton accompanied by chipped potatoes, red currant jelly, and any greens in season (and consequently cheap). Then offer a sweet and a jelly.

If you can, invest in a cheap freezer and give ices. Have made an ordinary boiled custard, flavour it with essence of vanilla or lemon and freeze it.

As regards the coffee, even if you can not afford the finest mocha, take care that the coffee is always well made, perfectly clear, free from grounds and served absolutely hot. In this way, people will remark upon its excellence, and even ask *'where you got it.'*

pennyworth
of
cream

As to wine, if you can not afford good port, burgundy, &c., do without, and a cheap claret or hock will suffice for the guests. Upon other occasions, when you are alone, drink either water, or the occasional glass of claret.

drink water

WAITING AT TABLE

Here is the secret to enable your two maids to wait at table:

The cook, with the parlourmaid's assistance, cooks the dinner. Have a charwoman in for the evening, who dishes up, and afterwards washes the dinner things and tidies up generally whilst the two maids are handing the coffee, &c. For this service, you can pay her one shilling and give her supper, but only requisition her services upon very special occasions.

pay one shilling and supper

A SMALL EVENING PARTY

Occasionally it will be necessary to give a small evening party. Try to limit the number of guests to thirty or thirty-five. Do not engage any waiters, first and foremost because of the costs and secondly, because most people dislike anything in the nature of false pretences and ostentation.

false pretences

If friends cared to come and see, they must take you and your house in its everyday apparel.

Anything in the nature of a sit-down supper is quite out of the question with a tiny dining-room and an even tinier housekeeping allowance.

NEVER A LUNCHEON PARTY!

A luncheon party means spending the money which ought to provide dinner, and therefore if you wish to ask anyone to share a meal with you, let that meal be dinner, not, most emphatically not, luncheon.

IN A MONEY BOX

Contrive to save a little out of the housekeeping money every week, sometimes two or three shillings, sometimes less. Put this away in a money-box, and the sum thus saved enables you to give an occasional entertainment.

AFTERNOON RECEPTION

At an afternoon reception, give only brown and white bread and butter, hot tea-cakes and a little plum cake, tea and coffee. Take care, however, that the tea-cakes are always freshly made and quite hot, and that the bread and butter is daintily cut.

freshly
made
tea-cakes

DRESS

If up to her marriage a young woman has always had everything bought for her, then the spending of the dress allowance will be a problem.

small dress allowance Take courage in both hands, and make up your mind that you will succeed and be well-dressed into the bargain. Take your allowance half-yearly, not quarterly, because to a woman with a small allowance there are two seasons, summer and winter.

Budget

Then proceed to mentally map out the budget. You probably have enough underlinen, white skirts, stockings, and fal-lals generally to last quite a long time. Be sure not to let these get low, and add to them, even before the stock needs replenishing.

What to wear to shop in
Decide to invest in one of the half guinea rough serge costumes in navy blue. This is one of the best colours for hard wear.

In summer discard the coat, except on chilly days, and wear the skirt with a cotton blouse. This gown should be kept solely for out-of-door wear.

best colours

Never invest in light-coloured or white shirts. Always select dark or butcher blue, with or without a white pin spot, or else bright scarlet, as these do not require such frequent washing as the pale pinks, blues, creams and whites.

Finery
Before indulging in any finery, purchase all the absolutely necessary things first, and then spend the residue, if any, on smart frocks and hats.

necessities first

77

Footwear

careful soling and heeling

Boots and shoes should claim attention next. For best, you can get a smart pair of patents for half-a-guinea, you will need a pair of stout calf red shoes, a pretty pair of court shoes, for evening wear, and a very fair pair of brown Oxford shoes. These shoes should last considerably longer than a year, by dint of careful soling and heeling.

a little woman

A little woman

Find some lengths of smart material for dresses at a sale and find a little woman whose charge for making is only half a guinea!

Hats

A really smart hat, and a smartly trimmed toque for second best, together with a sailor hat for morning wear, constitute millinery for the half-year.

For the evening
If you have been out so much that your evening
dresses are beginning to look sadly the worse for
wear, you can renovate a black bengaline, by means   renovate
of an overdress of sequinned net. Cheap satins, and
cheap common silks of the pseudo fashionable kind
are to be abhorred. If good ones are beyond reach,
do without any.

> Moral – Buy a length of good material, even if it is
> slightly unfashionable, in preference to a cheap and
> shoddy article of later date.

Stockings
You can not do with less than half a dozen pairs of
stockings.

Winter

When October comes you will have imperative need of a smart winter coat and half a dozen pairs of gloves. For every-day wear, on days when something warmer than a serge coat is needed, try a reversible golf cape in a bronze and scarlet tartan.

Under-linen

You must also allow for adding to under-linen; a moreen petticoat for every-day wear and corsets.

Trimmings

Now and again you will need to spend a few shillings, too, for evening gloves, a little lace or trimming to furbish up a gown. Do without any other extravagances. Veils run away with a by no means inconsiderable sum in a year, so avoid purchasing them.

Small items
Go carefully with pins and hairpins, and other small articles. Take good care that your servants do not make free with needles cottons, &c., for it is in these small ways that money is wasted and can be saved.

Colours
New colours have an ugly way of dating themselves, one is always safe with dark blue, black, grey, brown and mauve.

Never be tempted
So, one need not necessarily be dowdy on a small dress allowance; good taste will go farther than a great deal of cash injudiciously expended! Keep your eye out for a bargain and never be tempted by bargains solely because they are bargains.

bargains

Ways to be careful

Be careful with gowns. Always wear a dainty apron in the mornings when about your household duties. That stitch in time should never be neglected and always bear in mind that the markedly fashionable soon becomes the markedly unfashionable. Never invest in muslin gowns, these need a visit to the laundress after being worn two or three times. It is only the heroine of a novel who can hope to look well in a badly got up muslin gown.

a
stitch
in
time

AMUSEMENTS

There is no reason to degenerate into dullness on a small income. It is a good idea to form a common fund, and by saving all odd pence, accumulate enough for a trip to the theatre occasionally.
It is nothing short of wonderful how soon odd pence do mount up.

by
saving
odd
pence

The cost of travel
If you travel to a dance in a cab, you will arrive perfectly fresh and unrumpled. A thing one cannot hope for if travelling by bus or train.

Goloshes
When friends live within a walkable distance, wear goloshes over evening shoes. This saves the shoes and prevents them getting dusty.

THE ANNUAL HOLIDAY

'Pretty furnished cottage to be let. Four bedrooms, sitting room and kitchen, bracing locality, rent 10 shillings weekly.'

A cottage in the country

There are hundreds of cottages to be had in quaint unfrequented little places. However they may be situated a mile or two from a railway station.
One bedroom can be used by servants and one by friends who are also none too well off.

a
jolly
time

At the seaside
Rents are slightly higher at the seaside, but the excess is so very trifling that it will be found well worth your while to pay it if sea air suits you better than country. A jolly time can be had by all!

THE FAMILY MEDICINE CHEST

The importance of good health can not be over-rated, especially with regard to the mistress of a household.

Meals

The average woman with indifferent health has often only herself to thank for it. Take the daily meals for instance. She may eat a fairly good breakfast to start with, but of what does her luncheon often consist? A cup of overstrong tea and a piece of bread and butter of wafer-thinness, or an indigestible cream bun. This repast is repeated at five o'clock under the title of afternoon tea! Then she wonders why she feels ill, weak and out of sorts! A plateful of good Scotch broth and a roll can be had for sevenpence.

overstrong
tea

good
Scotch
broth

85

A *timely tonic*

A young wife may feel run down and generally debilitated in the Spring and wait on and on, hoping it will 'pass off', instead of going straight to a doctor at once. A timely tonic will save loads of chemist's stuff and is well worth the single five shillings which that visit would cost.

A *clean house*

well
flushed
and
sweet

A thoroughly clean house can not be an altogether unhealthy house, but no matter how clean the house itself may be, if the sinks, lavatories, &c., are not kept well flushed and sweet, especially in hot weather, illness may result therefrom.

A *good plan*

Once a week, every sink, lavatory, &c. in the house should be well flushed with chloride of lime water.

Greasy accumulations in the sink pipe are dispersed with hot water. Give ordinary drains a thorough flushing with hot and then cold water.

Hot water will cleanse away all impurities and leave the pipes in a much sweeter and cleaner condition than any amount of cold water could possibly do.

The dustbin

Too much importance also can not be attached to keeping the dustbin in good order and having it emptied at regular intervals. With regard to the dustbin, never allow vegetable refuse of any sort to be thrown into this.

the dustbin

Cooking smells

When greens are being boiled – (and to cook greens properly the lid of the saucepan should be off dur-

cedar powder

ing the cooking) – if a little cedar powder is thrown on the top of the stove, only the pleasant odour of the burnt cedar dust will be perceptible through the house instead of that too pungent bouquet. No small household should be without this really invaluable stuff.

Unsound food
Never buy unsound fruit or vegetables, even though the unsoundness consist of but the tiniest speck here and there.
Never buy, and certainly never cook, fish which you even suspect to be tainted, no matter how slightly.

Stale food of all sorts, with the one exception of bread, is bad for the health of both you and yours.

A *few remedies*

Every mistress of a household should possess:

remedies

A bottle of pure olive oil for burns.

A small bottle of carron oil (made by mixing linseed oil and limewater in equal proportions) as a remedy for scalds or burns.

A bottle of liquorice powder for use as an aperient.

A bottle of Epsom salts.

A bottle of embrocation for strained muscles.

A bottle of camphorated oil for rubbing into the chest for colds.

A bottle of citrate of magnesia, useful when a cooling drink is required.

A packet of mustard leaves, a packet of porous plasters, a shilling bottle of diarrhoea mixture and a bottle of brandy. *This latter should be kept in the medicine chest and should never be used on any pretext save that of illness.*

brandy

SOME HELPFUL HINTS

The economical cook always keeps parsley in the house. Buy a pennyworth every Saturday and keep it with the roots only in water; by this means it will last the whole week round if the water is changed every day.

You must give your stock a boiling up once a day if you wish it to keep sweet and fresh all the week round, and you must also wash the stock pot out thoroughly each time it has been used, and then rinse it well with cold water. If you omit this precaution your soup will sour.

A clove of garlic must be removed if it has been added to a recipe whole.

SOME HELPFUL HINTS

When you want to be very extravagant, a pennyworth or twopennyworth of cream added to a soup will be found a great improvement, but is by no means necessary.

To egg fish economically use a small brush. If these brushes are used with egging instead of the old fashioned wasteful mode of slapping the article to be cooked into the beaten egg, a single egg will suffice for both fish, and, say, a dish of cutlets.

Any scraps of cold beef which may be left from a joint should never be wasted. Free them from fat, pass through the mincing machine, and turn into Croquette de Boeuf.

SOME HELPFUL HINTS

 Never leave the fat to get cold in the saucepan when you have finished frying. Always empty it out through a clean gravy strainer into a clean bowl, and place the latter in a cool corner in the larder till next required.

 Shake the saucepan occasionally when frying, this will prevent the potatoes, or whatever the article in question may be, from sticking to the bottom and burning.

 An old fowl or a spring chicken?
An old fowl stewed, with plenty of time in which to cook, must be frequently basted and then will be found so tender as to be very little inferior to spring chicken.

SOME HELPFUL HINTS

Never have clear soup even when you have a dinner party, because this cannot be properly clarified without raw beef, and this adds to the expense.

When you have a dinner party, serve a well-made purée, and you will find that most people appreciate it, because it is a thing they do not get every day, whereas clear soup is a standing dish at every dinner-party one goes to.

Never buy things for which you have not an immediate and definite use, and, above all, never buy anything common. Better stuff a little out of date, really good, than the most up to date but cheap.

THE SERVANTLESS HOUSEHOLD
HOW TO COPE – SOME POLITE ADVICE
How to keep the house in order without
the benefit of staff. Maintain high stan-
dards and be prepared for anything!
Includes essential 'Don'ts and Buts'.

DAINTY DISHES
FOR SLENDER INCOMES

Do not be constrained by your budget.
Money-saving ideas, well-tried recipes
and 'hints worth remembering'.

KITCHEN COSMETICS
BEAUTY FROM YOUR PANTRY
How to have a smooth, clear complexion –
and other potions and preparations for
natural beauty.
Original ingredients from yesterday's
kitchens.

For your free catalogue containing these and other
titles write to:

Copper Beech Publishing
P O Box 159 East Grinstead
Sussex England RH19 4FS
www.copperbeechpublishing.co.uk

Copper Beech Gift Books
are designed and printed in
Great Britain.